anythink

Ferrets

Mia Bennett

PowerKiDS
press

New York

Published in 2018 by The Rosen Publishing Group, Inc.
29 East 21st Street, New York, NY 10010

First Edition

Editor: Melissa Raé Shofner
Book Design: Rachel Rising

Photo Credits: Cover Timolina/Shutterstock.com; Cover, p.1 Couperfield/Shutterstock.com; pp. 4, 22 Eric Isselee/Shutterstock.com; p. 5 Tim Graham/Getty Images News/Getty Images; p. 7 Bob Bennett/Getty Images; p. 9 Fayzulin Serg/Shutterstock.com; p. 11 Best dog photo/Shutterstock.com; p. 13 Xseon/Shutterstock.com; p. 14 Dmitrij Skorobogatov/Shutterstock.com; p. 15 Burden Iliya/Shutterstock.com; p. 17 Yanik Chauvin/Shutterstock.com; p. 19 Miroslav Hlavko/Shutterstock.com; p. 20 vandycan/Shutterstock.com; p. 21 safonovaolga/Shutterstock.com.

Cataloging-in-Publication Data
Names: Bennett, Mia.
Title: Ferrets / Mia Bennett.
Description: New York : PowerKids Press, 2018. | Series: Our weird pets | Includes index.
Identifiers: ISBN 9781508154228 (pbk.) | ISBN 9781508154167 (library bound) | ISBN 9781508154044 (6 pack)
Subjects: LCSH: Ferret–Juvenile literature. | Ferrets as pets–Juvenile literature.
Classification: LCC QL737.C25 B46 2018 | DDC 636.976'628–dc23

Manufactured in the United States of America

CPSIA Compliance Information: Batch #BS17PK: For Further Information contact Rosen Publishing, New York, New York at 1-800-237-9932

Contents

Smelly Little Thieves

Ferrets are one of the most popular pets in the United States. These small, furry animals make great companions. They are fun and playful pets that sometimes get into trouble for stealing things. In fact, their Latin name means "smelly little thief."

Ferrets were likely **domesticated** thousands of years ago. They're easy to train, and they love to run. Ferrets were once used for hunting small animals, such as rabbits and **rodents**. Today, ferrets sometimes help people by pulling wire through underground tunnels or cleaning pipes.

PET FOOD FOR THOUGHT

A group of ferrets is called a business!

In England, people take their ferrets to special racing events and watch them run through tubes.

In the Wild

Ferrets are part of the weasel family. Otters and badgers are also members of this family. Domesticated ferrets are meant to be pets, but their close relatives live in the wild.

Wild black-footed ferrets live in North America. They have black fur around their eyes and on their feet. They mostly eat prairie dogs. Wild ferrets tend to sleep much of the day and spend their nights hunting. They creep into prairie dog **burrows** to hunt.

PET FOOD FOR THOUGHT

In the 1880s, hundreds of ferrets were released, or let go, into the wild in New Zealand. They're now a danger to native wildlife there.

Black-footed ferrets are **endangered**. There are only around 300 left in the wild.

7

Ferret Features

What do ferrets look like? They're small **mammals**, even smaller than cats. They usually weigh less than 5 pounds (2.3 kg). Their long, thin bodies help them fit into tight spaces. They may have been domesticated for their ability to hunt rodents. They can easily follow rodents into underground burrows.

Ferrets come in many colors. Albino ferrets are white with pink eyes. Many ferrets have a mix of brown and cream-colored fur. Others have fur that is black or gray.

PET FOOD FOR THOUGHT

Some people think ferrets are related to rodents, such as rats, but they aren't!

Ferrets have sharp teeth and claws. They use their claws for digging.

9

Home Sweet Home

In the wild, black-footed ferrets live in tunnels that used to belong to prairie dogs. They also find homes in burrows left behind by other animals.

If you keep a ferret as a pet, it will probably spend most of its day sleeping in a cage. However, it needs time to run around outside its cage. Ferrets tend to sleep a lot, but they have a lot of energy when awake. They live best in warm places between 50° and 80° Fahrenheit (10° and 26.7° Celsius).

PET FOOD FOR THOUGHT

Ferrets are great escape artists. Their cage should have a good lock. The openings between the cage bars should be small.

Ferrets like cages that have more than one level. Some cages have stairs, slopes, and landings.

Feeding Your Ferret

Ferrets are carnivores, or animals that eat only meat. Because of that, you need to feed your pet ferret food that's high in **protein**. Many people purchase special high-protein ferret food. Other people feed their ferrets raw or cooked chicken.

Ferrets need to eat many times throughout the day. They burn off the food they eat very quickly. You can give your ferret snacks such as cooked eggs or meat. Ferrets should not eat fruits, vegetables, dairy, or sugar.

PET FOOD FOR THOUGHT

A ferret's sharp teeth are one clue that it's a meat eater.

Feeding a ferret is a lot like feeding a cat. They need meat-based food, and they love treats!

13

Happy and Healthy

How can you keep your ferret happy and healthy? Ferrets live for about 6 to 13 years. Just like cats and dogs, they need to have **vaccinations** to stay healthy. Ferrets can get **parasites** such as fleas and heartworm. Vaccinations and other care can keep illnesses and parasites away.

Ferrets love to sleep for most of the day—sometimes up to 22 hours! Keep your ferret happy by giving it lots of time to play and explore your home.

PET FOOD FOR THOUGHT

Ferrets use litter boxes like cats. Keep its litter clean to keep your ferret happy!

Take your ferret to the vet at least once a year for a checkup.

15

Ferret Personalities

Ferrets are very curious and playful animals. They're social, which means they like to play with other ferrets. They'll also play with other small animals, such as cats, but they should always be **supervised**.

Ferrets are very smart. You can train them to do simple tasks and use a litter box. Ferrets can also figure out puzzle games. They like toys that move and make noise. Most of all, ferrets love to run through tunnels and tubes.

PET FOOD FOR THOUGHT

Ferrets are known to steal things such as keys and other small objects. They're always up to **mischief**!

Ferrets like to **wrestle** and play with other ferrets. They even play games of "hide and seek."

Be Careful!

Ferrets have a bad **reputation** because they sometimes hurt small children. It's true that some ferrets may bite children. However, this often happens because a child hurts their pet or holds it incorrectly.

It's important to always stay calm and be gentle when playing with a ferret. Never drop or hit your ferret. Some ferrets need to be trained to play gently, as they might think it's OK to wrestle and bite.

PET FOOD FOR THOUGHT

Ferrets may live best in a household with children over the age of 12.

Every ferret is different. It's important to understand what makes your ferret comfortable and uncomfortable.

19

Ferret Friends

Ferrets are fun and friendly pets. These mischievous thieves and tunnel runners are also a little bit unusual. Do you think you're ready to add a ferret to your home?

Make sure you have enough time to spend with your ferret. Make sure your house is ferret proof. Ferrets can get into a lot of trouble and creep into small spaces. Most of all, expect mischief and a bit of a smell from your ferret. They are, of course, smelly little thieves.

If you give your ferret love and attention, it will be your friend for life!

21

Ferret Care Fact Sheet

- Ferrets need tall cages with bars that are close together.

- Give your ferret things to climb on and hide in, such as boxes and tubes.

- Ferrets need lots of protein to eat and water to drink.

- Ferrets sleep most of the day.

- Ferrets love to play, run around, and explore.

- Clean your ferret's cage once a week.

- Scoop your ferret's litter box once a day.

- Handle your ferret carefully and hold it gently.

Glossary

burrow: A hole in the ground an animal uses to live in or hide in.

domesticated: Bred and raised for use by people.

endangered: In danger of dying out.

mammal: A warm-blooded animal that has a backbone and hair, breathes air, and feeds milk to its young.

mischief: A playful desire to cause trouble.

parasite: A living thing that lives in, on, or with another living thing, causing harm.

protein: A nutrient in many types of food that the body uses to grow, repair tissues, and stay healthy.

reputation: The views that are held about someone or something.

rodent: A small, furry animal with large front teeth, such as a mouse or rat.

supervise: To watch over.

vaccination: The injection of weakened or dead microorganisms to build up the immune system against a disease.

wrestle: To take part in a fight, often in play, that includes trying to force someone or something else to the ground.

Index

Websites

Due to the changing nature of Internet links, PowerKids Press has developed an online list of websites related to the subject of this book. This site is updated regularly. Please use this link to access the list: www.powerkidslinks.com/owp/ferr